D0734393

HOME
REPAIRS

DO - IT - YOURSELF

HOME
REPAIRS

David Holloway

LORENZ BOOKS

This edition is published by Lorenz Books,
an imprint of Anness Publishing Ltd,
Blaby Road,
Wigston,
Leicestershire LE18 4SE;

info@anness.com

www.lorenzbooks.com;
www.annesspublishing.com

If you like the images in this book and
would like to investigate using them for
publishing, promotions or advertising,
please visit our website
www.practicalpictures.com for more
information.

Publisher: Joanna Lorenz
Editors: Felicity Forster, Anne Hildyard
Photographer: John Freeman
Illustrator: Andrew Green
Designer: Bill Mason
Production Controller: Mai-Ling Collyer

Additional text: Catherine Tully

ACKNOWLEDGEMENTS AND NOTES
The publisher would like to
thank The Tool Shop for supplying
tools for jacket photography:
97 Lower Marsh
Waterloo, London SE1 7AB
Tel 020 7207 2077; Fax 020 7207 5222
www.thetoolshop-diy.com

The author and publishers have made
every effort to ensure that all instructions
contained within this book are accurate
and safe, and cannot accept liability for
any resulting injury, damage or loss to
persons or property, however it may arise.
If in any doubt as to the correct procedure
to follow for any home improvements
task, seek professional advice.

CONTENTS

INTRODUCTION

Where your home is concerned, prevention is often better, and certainly less expensive, than cure. A regular programme of inspection and maintenance will prevent small problems from becoming large and costly ones. From time to time, however, repairs will be necessary, and their successful completion depends on having all the relevant tools and equipment to hand, and understanding how to use them.

This book will guide you through a wide range of common repairs that may be needed to walls, ceilings, doors, windows, floors and stairs, showing you a variety of simple techniques for achieving professional results. By following its advice, and applying a little forethought, care and patience, you will not only save money, but will also have the satisfaction of knowing that you have done the jobs yourself. Moreover, the basic skills you learn will provide a core of knowledge that should give you the confidence to tackle more ambitious do-it-yourself projects.

When beginning a repair job, be sure that everything is to hand; it is no use beginning to repair a wall, then finding that you are too short to reach the top and that you need to go looking for a trestle or a pair of steps. All your tools and equipment should be well prepared and in position.

LEFT: A beautiful home will only stay that way if it is well looked after. Sooner or later, however, repairs will be necessary; the various tasks shown on the following pages will help you to keep your home looking pristine.

THE RIGHT CLOTHING

Overalls are a good investment because they not only protect clothing, but are also designed to be close-fitting to prevent accidental contact with moving machinery. Industrial gloves can provide very useful protection against cuts and bruises when doing rough jobs, such as removing broken glass from windows, lifting floorboards and chiselling out damaged ceramic tiles. Similarly, safety boots should be worn for heavy lifting or when the use of machinery is involved.

ABOVE: Rubber knee pads for floor work avoid damage to both floor and worker.

Knee pads are necessary for comfort when laying a floor, stripping one for varnishing or carrying out any other job that requires a lot of kneeling. They will also protect the wearer from injury if a nail or similar projection is knelt on accidentally. Finally, a bump cap is worth considering. This will protect the head from minor injuries and bumps, but is not so cumbersome as the hard hat required on building sites.

ABOVE: Wear overalls for protection when painting and decorating.

ABOVE: Safety boots with steel toe caps will protect your feet.

FIRST AID

It is inevitable that minor cuts and abrasions will occur at some point, so a basic first aid kit is another essential for the home or workshop. Keep your kit in a prominent position ready for use. If any of the contents are used, replace them immediately.

first aid kit

AIRBORNE DANGERS

When you are working with wood, the most common airborne danger is dust, mainly from sawing and sanding. This can do long-term damage to the lungs. Many do-it-yourself enthusiasts do not do enough work to warrant a portable dust extractor, but it would be worth considering if funds allowed. Such a device can be moved around the house to suit any tool in use and it would be very useful if a home workshop was contemplated.

A simple face mask, however, will offer adequate protection for occasional jobs.

These can also be purchased for protection against fumes, such as from solvents, which can be very harmful.

dust mask

Dust, of course, also affects the eyes, so it is worth investing in a pair of impact-resistant goggles, which will protect the wearer from both fine dust and flying debris. Full facial protection is available in the form of a powered respirator for those working in dusty conditions over long periods.

ELECTRICAL SAFETY

To safeguard against electrocution, which can occur if the flex (power cord) is faulty or is cut accidentally, the ideal precaution is a residual current device (RCD). This is simply plugged into the main supply socket (electrical outlet) before the flex and will give complete protection to the user. Extension leads can be purchased with automatic safety cutouts and insulated sockets, and are ideal for both outside and inside work.

The danger of electrocution or damage caused by accidentally drilling into an existing cable or pipe can be largely prevented by using an electronic pipe and cable detector. This will locate and differentiate between metal pipes, wooden studs and live wires through plaster and concrete to a depth of approximately 50mm (2in). They are not too expensive and will be very useful around the home.

LEFT: A simple circuit breaker can save a life.

SAFE ACCESS

Steps and ladders can be hazardous, so make sure they are in good condition. Accessories to make a ladder safer to use include a roof hook, which slips over the ridge for safety; a ladder stay, which spreads the weight of the ladder across a vertical surface, such as a wall, to prevent slippage; and a standing platform, which is used to provide a more comfortable and safer surface to stand on. The last often has a ribbed rubber surface and can be attached to the rungs of almost all ladders.

Even more stable is a movable workstation or a board or staging slung between two pairs of steps or trestles. This can often be used with a safety rail, which will prevent you from falling even if you do slip.

ABOVE: A movable workstation simplifies the whole process.

ABOVE: Platforms supported by trestles are a safe way to paint at a height.

TIPS

• Never over-reach when working on steps or a ladder; climb down and reposition it.
• Never allow children or pets into areas where power tools or strong solvents are being used.
• Do not work when you are overtired. This causes lapses in concentration, which can lead to silly and/or dangerous mistakes.
• Keep the work environment tidy. Flexes (power cords) should not be walked on or coiled up tightly, because it damages them internally. Moreover, trailing flexes can be a trip hazard, and long extension leads can be prone to overheating.

USING PROFESSIONALS

As a do-it-yourself enthusiast, you have to be familiar with several trades, but it is often well worth employing a professional for structural work to save time and possibly money. There are many jobs, especially in plumbing and electrics, where professional help is welcome and indeed necessary. Professionals can also advise you in advance if your project is likely to fail for a reason you may not even have considered.

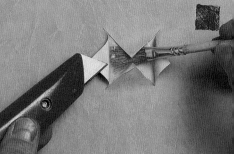

TOOLS & MATERIALS

Most tool kits grow organically as specific tools are added when the need arises. The tools featured on the following pages show a useful selection to have for repair and maintenance work. If your budget is tight, it is best to buy several hand tools rather than one power tool. This has the benefit of improving your manual skills at an early stage, which will give encouraging results as well as increase the range of jobs you can undertake. You will also need a range of materials, such as nails, screws and drill bits. These come in an array of shapes and sizes, so need to be selected carefully. Finally, a few basic adhesives and sealants are needed for many repair jobs. They can make all the difference when used correctly.

TOOLS

Measuring and marking out are common tasks. A retractable steel measuring tape will take care of the former, while a combination square will allow you to mark cutting lines at 90 and 45 degrees. A craft knife can be used for marking the cutting lines as well as for cutting soft sheet materials.

A spirit (carpenter's) level is essential for finding a true horizontal or vertical.

For driving nails, a claw hammer is the ideal general-purpose tool, but for small pins (brads), the narrow end of a cross-pein hammer is better. You will need a nail punch to punch nail heads below the surface of the work, and a nail puller to remove nails or pins.

Various sizes of screwdriver for slotted, Phillips and Pozidriv screws will be necessary, while an adjustable spanner can be used on nuts, bolts and pipe fittings.

G-clamps are useful for holding items together temporarily while permanent fixings are made.

Saws are also essential. Choose a general-purpose hand saw for large sections of wood and a tenon saw for smaller work. A mitre box will allow you to make 45-degree cuts.

For drilling holes, a cordless drill will be most convenient.

Use a jack plane for shaping wood, and bevel-edged chisels to make cutouts and recesses. Abrasive paper is essential for giving a final finish to wood.

When filling cracks and holes, use a putty knife for small repairs and a small trowel for larger ones.

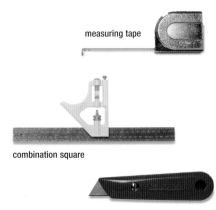

measuring tape

combination square

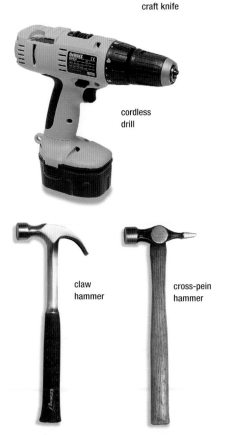

craft knife

cordless drill

claw hammer

cross-pein hammer

hand saw

G-clamp

tenon saw

mitre box

spirit
(carpenter's)
level

adjustable
spanner

abrasive
papers

small
trowel

jack plane

nail punch

nail puller

putty knife

screwdrivers

bevel-edged chisel

NAILS, SCREWS AND DRILL BITS

There is no such thing as an "ordinary" nail. All nails have been designed for specific purposes, although some can be put to several uses.

Wire, lost-head and oval nails can be used for general carpentry. Oval nails can be driven below the surface of the work with less likelihood of them splitting the wood.

Cut nails have a tapering, rectangular section, which gives them excellent holding properties. They are largely used for fixing flooring.

Panel pins (brads) are used for fixing thin panels and cladding. They are nearly always punched below the surface, as are veneer pins.

When there is a need to secure thin or fragile sheet material, such as plasterboard (gypsum board), large-headed nails are used. These are commonly called clout nails, but may also be found under specific names, such as plasterboard nails.

The holding power of screws is much greater than that of nails, and items that have been screwed together can easily be taken apart again without damage to the components.

There are various types of screw head, the most common being the slotted screw head, followed by the Phillips head and the Pozidriv head, both of which have a cruciform pattern to take the screwdriver blade.

Drill bits come in a bewildering array of sizes and types but only a few are needed by the do-it-yourselfer, such as dowel bits for flat-bottomed holes, flat bits, which cut large holes very rapidly, and twist bits, which make small holes and are used for starting screws.

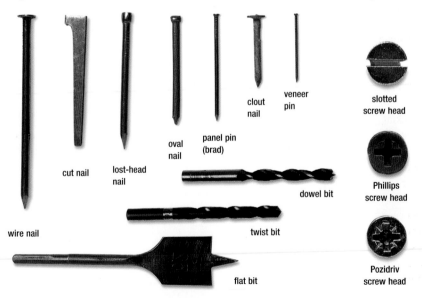

cut nail

lost-head nail

wire nail

oval nail

panel pin (brad)

clout nail

veneer pin

dowel bit

twist bit

flat bit

slotted screw head

Phillips screw head

Pozidriv screw head

ADHESIVES AND SEALANTS

A fantastic range of adhesives and sealants is available, some designed for specific uses, woodworking adhesive and bath sealant for example, and others formulated for general use. It is a good idea to keep a selection of both adhesives and sealants in your do-it-yourself armoury, so that you have them to hand in the event of an emergency repair situation.

The majority of woodworking jobs that require two or more pieces of wood to be glued together need wood glue or a PVA (white) glue. This white liquid dries quickly, loses its colour, and excess adhesive can be removed with a damp cloth before it sets.

Two-part epoxy resin adhesives can be used on a wide range of materials. The two parts come in separate tubes and must be mixed together just before use.

Superglue has the advantage of setting almost immediately, so you can actually hold the two parts to be glued rather than fitting clamps.

The majority of sealants come in cartridges designed to fit into a caulking gun. This is an essential, but inexpensive, tool and is easy to use after a little practice. One of the most useful sealants for use around the home is a white waterproof sealant, which can be used to fill the gap between a bath, basin or shower tray and a wall. Gap-filling sealants can be used for sealing between two materials that are likely to move slightly, such as gaps around a door frame.

wood glue

superglue

two-part epoxy resin adhesive

gap-filling sealant

ABOVE: Use white waterproof sealant for the gap behind a washbasin. Apply it in one movement.

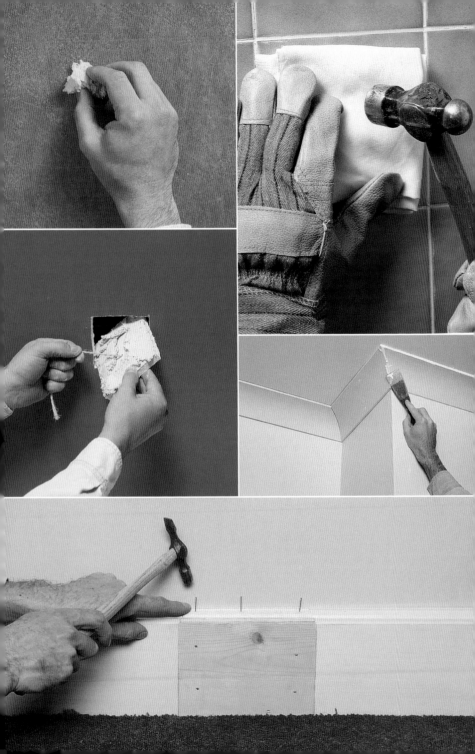

WALLS & CEILINGS

Most walls and ceilings have some form of plaster surface, whether it be plaster on a backing of wooden laths or plasterboard (gypsum board) on a wooden framework. This rigid material may suffer from cracking and damage due to building settlement or accidental impact. Fortunately, this is relatively easy to repair, either with a filler material or a plasterboard patch. Walls also feature wooden skirtings (baseboards) and decorative architraves (trims) around door openings. These, too, can become damaged and may need repairing or replacing. Wallpapering problems such as air bubbles, tears and gaps are easily fixed, as are the jobs of removing and replacing broken ceramic wall tiles.

PREPARATION AND MINOR REPAIRS

Walls and ceilings need to be prepared carefully so that the surfaces are in as good a condition as possible. The better the surface, the better the new finish.

If the room was papered originally, the first job is to remove all the old wallcovering. With vinyl, it should be possible to peel off the outer layer to leave the backing behind. If this is in good condition, you can paper over it again, but if you wish to paint the walls, it should be removed too.

Painted surfaces can be painted over, but make sure that any loose or flaking paint is removed first. Then you can begin to repair any cracks or other damage in the surfaces.

A general-purpose filler can be used for the majority of cracks in ceilings and walls. This comes ready-mixed in tubs or as a powder for mixing with water. Simply apply the filler with a filling or putty knife, pressing it into the cracks and smoothing it flush with the surface. Some cracks need enlarging slightly to give the filler something to grip; fine cracks can be filled with special hairline crack filler.

Normal fillers are quite adequate if you are papering the ceiling or wall, but for paint, a fine surface filler is better. Most fillers take a short while to dry, after which they can be sanded flush with the surrounding surface.

1 Strip wallcoverings by soaking them with water or by using a steam stripper, then remove with scrapers. Peel off the top layer of vinyl types to leave the backing behind.

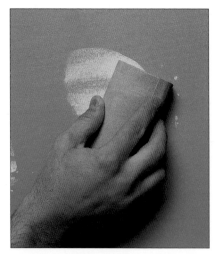

4 When dry, sand the filled area smooth with fine abrasive paper. On flat surfaces, wrap the abrasive paper around a sanding block. You may need to add more filler to fill any remaining defects.

2 Remove flaking paint with a scraper. Take care not to dig the blade into soft surfaces. Feather the edges of the sound paint by sanding lightly. This will disguise them under the new finish.

3 Fill any cracks and gaps in plasterwork with all-purpose filler. Press the filler firmly into the gap and finish off by leaving it slightly proud of the surrounding surface.

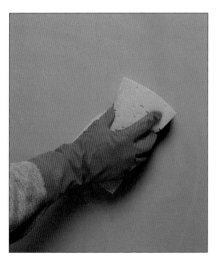

5 Give the walls a thorough wash with a solution of sugar soap (all-purpose cleaner). This will remove all dust and grease. Allow the liquid to dry completely before decorating the wall.

6 Using a squeegee mop to clean ceilings will allow you to work at ground level. Make sure you spread dust sheets (drop cloths) on the floor to protect it from drips.

FILLING HOLES IN PLASTER

Small holes, especially those left by screws, can be filled in the same way as cracks. Cut off any protruding wall plugs or, better still, remove them altogether so that you can obtain a smooth finish.

Larger holes are more of a problem. The kind of hole left by removing a waste pipe from a wall can be made good with do-it-yourself repair plaster, which can usually be applied in layers up to 50mm (2in) thick. Smaller recesses up to 20mm (¾in) deep can be treated with a special deep-gap filler, while really deep cavities can be filled with an expanding foam filler. Once set, this can be cut and sanded smooth, then painted or papered over. If an area of plaster has fallen off the wall, use a repair plaster, levelling it with the surrounding sound plaster with a straight length of wood.

For larger areas, nail wooden battens to the wall. These should be equal in depth to the surrounding original plaster. By running a long wooden straightedge up the battens, using a sawing action, you will be able to level off the fresh plaster to the correct depth. When the plaster has set partially, the battens can be prised from the wall and the resulting gaps in the plaster filled.

You may need to divide a really large area of wall into workable "bays" using this technique.

ABOVE: Use a paintbrush to remove dust from holes and deep cracks prior to filling, then rinse and work the damp bristles into the hole. This will prevent moisture from being sucked from the filler, which would cause it to dry too quickly, weakening it and leading to poor adhesion.

ABOVE: Use a repair plaster for a deep hole, applied with a plasterer's trowel. Work the plaster well into the hole and smooth it off flush with the surrounding surface. Allow to dry slightly, then polish smooth with a wet trowel.

REPAIRING LATH-AND-PLASTER

Holes in lath-and-plaster ceilings and walls can be repaired in the same way as holes in normal plastered surfaces, provided the laths are intact.

First brush the laths with diluted PVA (white) glue to reduce absorbency, then repair with general-purpose filler, deep-gap filler or repair plaster.

If the laths have broken, cut back the plaster until you expose the vertical studs. Cut a piece of plasterboard (gypsum board) to size and nail it in place before filling the hole.

If the damage covers a large area, it may be necessary to nail battens between the studs or joists to support the long edges of the patch. Nail them in place so that the nails project halfway into the opening.

This sort of repair can also be made using expanded aluminium mesh to support the repair plaster.

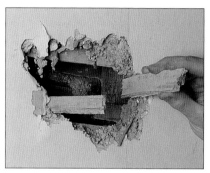

1 If the wood laths are split or broken, pull them away from the surface. Remove any loose sections of plaster.

2 Continue cutting back the old plaster and the laths behind it to expose the studs or ceiling joists at each side of the hole. Square off the edges.

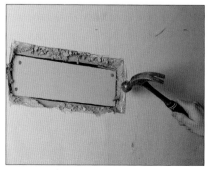

3 Cut a plasterboard patch to fit the hole, and nail it in place. Add two support strips if the panel is large.

4 Complete the repair by plastering over the patch after filling and taping the cut edges all around. Polish the repair with a steel float.

REPAIRING PLASTERBOARD

Surface damage and small holes in plasterboard (gypsum board) can be repaired in the same way as cracks and holes in solid plaster, but if a large hole has been punched in the material – by a door handle, for example – a different solution is required. In this case, a patch must be placed behind the hole to provide support for a layer of filler.

First, use a padsaw to open out the hole, squaring the sides. Then cut a section of fresh plasterboard to a length slightly less than the diagonal dimension of the hole. This will allow you to pass it through the hole at an angle. Drill a tiny hole in the middle of the plasterboard patch and pass a piece of knotted string through it before adding filler or coving (crown molding) adhesive to the edges on the grey side of the plasterboard. This will secure it firmly to the back of the existing plasterboard panel.

Pass the patch through the hole and pull it back against the edges. Hold the string taut while adding filler to the hole, then leave this to set. Cut off the projecting string and make good with a final smooth coat of general-purpose filler or finish plaster, ensuring the surface is level.

If the area of damage in a plasterboard wall or ceiling is substantial, it is

1 Use a padsaw to square up a hole in damaged plasterboard (gypsum board). Keep the size of the hole to the minimum necessary to accommodate the damaged plasterboard.

much more sensible to work back to the nearest studs or joists, using a padsaw to cut the cladding flush with the wood. Then nail 50mm (2in) square noggings between the studs or joists so that they project halfway into the opening. Nail 50 x 25mm (2 x 1in) battens to the studs or joists, flush with the faces of the noggings.

Cut a patch of plasterboard to fill the opening and nail this to the noggings and battens, using galvanized plasterboard nails.

Apply a layer of filler around the edges of the patch, bedding jointing tape into it as you go. Feather the edges with a damp sponge and apply another layer when it has dried to leave a perfect surface.

2 Attach a piece of string to the patch, knotting it at the back so that it cannot be pulled through the hole. It may help to insert a galvanized nail through the knot for extra security.

3 Butter the back of the patch with a layer of filler or coving (crown molding) adhesive, making sure the edges are covered and keeping the free end of the string out of the way.

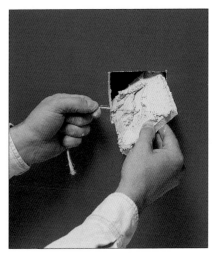

4 Pass the plasterboard patch through the hole while holding the free end of the string. Use the string to pull the patch firmly against the back of the existing plasterboard surface.

5 Add more filler or repair plaster to the hole while holding the patch tightly in place with the string. Leave the filler just below the surface of the wall and add a final thin layer when it has set.

REPLACING SKIRTING BOARDS

Skirtings (baseboards) protect wall surfaces at floor level from accidental damage. They can be plain or ornate, and can be painted, stained or varnished. They may need replacing if they are damaged or simply look unfashionable.

Skirtings are often fixed directly to masonry walls with large cut nails in older homes, or with masonry nails in more recent ones. Alternatively, they may be nailed to rough timber fixing blocks or grounds (furrings), which are themselves nailed to the masonry. Boards fixed to blocks are much easier to remove than those nailed directly to the wall, since both cut and masonry nails can have a ferocious grip. In the latter situation, it is often easier to punch the nails through the boards and into the walls than to try to prise them out. Boards on wood-framed walls are simply nailed to the frame and are easy to remove.

Provided the correct profile is available, small lengths of skirting can be replaced by levering the damaged section from the wall with a crowbar (wrecking bar), holding it clear of the wall with wooden wedges and sawing down through the moulding at each side of the damage with a tenon saw. For best results, the cuts should be made at 45 degrees with the aid of a mitre box, and the ends of the new piece cut in the same manner so that they overlap. Nails should be driven through the overlaps into wooden supporting blocks behind.

1 To replace a small area of damaged skirting (baseboard), prise it away from the wall slightly, wedge it and use a tenon saw and mitre box to cut out a section.

4 Nail the replacement board to the support blocks. If using plain wood, pin (tack) on decorative mouldings to build up a close match to the existing board.

2 Nail small support blocks behind the cut ends of the board, using masonry nails in brick and block walls, and then nail the cut ends to the support blocks.

3 Cut a piece of replacement board to fit, with its ends mitred to match the cut ends of the original board. Use plain wood if the skirting profile cannot be matched.

5 When replacing whole lengths, use mitre joints at external corners. Fix the first length, then mark the inside of the mitre on the back of the next board.

6 Cut the mitre joints with a power saw. At internal corners, fit the first length right into the corner. Then scribe its profile on to the second board; cut this with a coping saw, and fit it.

REPLACING ARCHITRAVES

Architraves (trims) are used around door and window openings to frame the opening and disguise the joint between the frame and the wall surface. Like skirtings (baseboards), they may need replacing if they are damaged or unfashionable.

Architraves are pinned (tacked) in place to the edges of the door or window frame. It is an easy job to prise the trims away with a bolster (stonecutter's) chisel without causing undue damage to the frame or the surrounding wall surface.

Once the old architrave has been removed, the edges of the wooden lining of the opening should be tidied up by scraping off ridges of old paint and filler.

Take careful measurements when cutting the new architrave, bearing in mind that mitred joints are normally used where the uprights meet the horizontal section above the opening.

If the new moulding is particularly ornate, it could be difficult to obtain neat joints, and you may prefer to add decorative corner blocks instead. These could also be fitted at the bottoms of the uprights if they are narrower than the originals and will not meet the skirtings (baseboards).

Fit the new sections of architrave 6mm (¼in) back from the edges of the lining of the opening.

1 Prise off the old mouldings. They should come away easily. If necessary, lever against a wooden block to avoid damaging the wall.

4 Fix the uprights to the frame by driving in nails at 300mm (12in) intervals. Recess the heads with a nail punch and fill the holes later.

2 Hold an upright against the frame so that the inside of the mitre joint can be marked on it. Repeat for the other upright.

3 Cut the end of the moulding, using a mitre block or box. Alternatively, mark the line across the moulding with a protractor or combination square.

5 Hold the top piece above the two uprights to mark the position for the mitre cut at each end. Make the cuts as before and test the piece for fit.

6 Nail the top piece to the frame, checking that the mitre joints are aligned accurately. Then drive a nail through each corner to secure the joint.

HIDING CEILING-TO-WALL JOINTS

Coving (crown molding), a quadrant-shaped moulding made from polystyrene, plaster or wood can be fitted between the walls and ceiling of a room. It has two functions: to be decorative and to conceal unsightly joints between the walls and ceiling. An ornate coving may be referred to as a cornice; old plaster cornices may be clogged with several layers of paint and need cleaning to reveal the detail.

Coving normally comes in long lengths and you will find it easier to fit if you have someone on hand to help place it in position. Where lengths meet at corners, the ends should be mitred for neat joints. The manufacturer may provide a cutting template; if not, use a large mitre box.

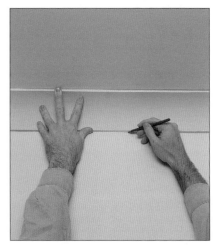

1 Mark guidelines on the ceiling and wall, using the dimensions given by the manufacturer. Alternatively, use a length of coving as a guide, but take care always to hold it at the same angle.

PREPARING LENGTHS OF COVING

1 Measure the coving required for each run and cut it to length with a fine-toothed saw. Mitre the ends, using a large mitre box, where they will meet at internal and external corners.

2 Mix enough adhesive for one length of coving at a time, otherwise it may become unusable. Butter the back edges of the coving with a liberal amount of adhesive.

2 Using the point of a trowel, score the surface of the ceiling and wall between the parallel lines. This will provide a key for the adhesive, ensuring a good grip.

3 Press the coving into place, aligning it carefully with the guidelines. Support the coving with nails driven partially into the wall below its bottom edge; remove them when the adhesive has set.

4 Continue the coving on the adjacent wall, carefully aligning the mitred ends of the two lengths. Any slight gaps between them can be filled later.

5 Complete the external corner with another length of coving, butting the ends together. Fill any gaps at external and internal angles with cellulose filler and sand down once dry.

REPAIRING WALLPAPER

Inadequate preparation and poor papering techniques, rather than faults with the paper itself, are the cause of most wallpapering problems. Some minor mistakes are quite easy to remedy, as shown here, but if the problem is extensive, it is better to strip off the affected area and start again.

AIR BUBBLES

Bubbles that remain after the paste has dried are caused by not allowing the paper to soak for long enough, not having brushed out the paper properly, or by poor preparation, which prevents the paper from sticking to the wall. Cut a cross in the bubble with a knife, apply paste to the underside of the paper and smooth on to the wall.

TEARS

If the tear is small, apply some overlap adhesive to the torn piece and ease it into place with the tips of a brush.

When faced with a large tear in wallpaper, remove loose and damaged paper by tearing it gently from the wall. Tear, rather than cut, a patch from a new piece of paper so that the pattern matches the surrounding area, then feather the edge by tearing away a 6mm (¼in) strip from the back. Paste the patch and lightly brush it into place.

With a vinyl wallcovering, cut a patch so that the pattern matches the surrounding area and tape it over the damage. Cut through both layers to form a square, remove the damaged vinyl, then paste and fit the patch.

EXPELLING AIR BUBBLES

1 Make diagonal cuts in an air bubble with a sharp knife, making sure they extend to the very edges of the bubble. Carefully bend the triangular flaps of paper back.

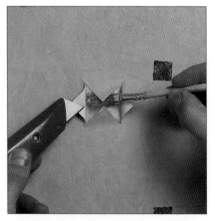

2 Mix up a little wallpaper adhesive and use a small, clean paintbrush to apply it beneath the cut flaps of paper. Press down each flap firmly and wipe off excess adhesive with a damp cloth.

REPAIRING TORN WALLCOVERINGS

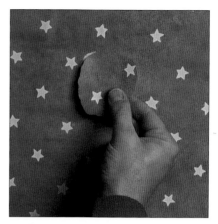

1 If it is not possible to paste a torn piece of paper back into place, carefully tear away all the loose or damaged wallpaper, feathering the edges all round.

2 Make a patch to cover the damage by carefully tearing, rather than cutting, the paper. Feather the edges. Paste the patch in place, making sure that you align the pattern.

REPAIRING VINYL

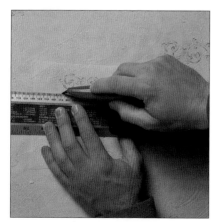

1 If a vinyl wallcovering is damaged, tape a new piece over the top, aligning the pattern. Then use a sharp knife and straightedge to cut through both patch and original covering in one go.

2 Remove the taped vinyl together with the damaged area of wallcovering. The new patch will fit the cutout exactly. Apply adhesive to the patch and press it into place.

OTHER PAPERING REPAIRS

Decorative paper finishes can suffer from a number of problems. Here are some of the most common ones and their cures.

GAPS IN SEAMS

Paper shrinking as it dries, due to poor pasting technique or poor butt joins, can cause gaps at the seams. Disguise the gaps with a felt-tipped pen in a similar shade to the base colour.

CURLING EDGES

These are caused by inadequate pasting, paste drying out during hanging or, on overlapped vinyl, the wrong paste having been used. Lift the edge of the paper with the back of a knife blade and apply a small amount of paste with a fine brush. Smooth the paper firmly into place with a damp sponge. For overlapping edges on vinyl wallpaper, use vinyl overlap adhesive.

SHINY PATCHES

Brushing matt finish wallpapers too vigorously can cause shiny patches. Normally, they cannot be removed, but rubbing gently with a piece of fresh white bread may disguise them. Bread is also useful for removing greasy fingermarks from non-washable papers.

> ### TIP
>
> Decorating equipment that has not been well cared for may spoil wallpaper. Wash all equipment and dry it well.

ABOVE: Disguise gaps with a felt-tipped pen, a crayon or watercolour paint.

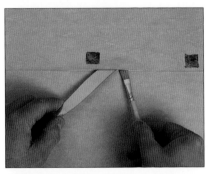

ABOVE: Apply wallpaper adhesive to curling edges with a fine brush.

ABOVE: Rubbing with a ball of white bread may make shiny patches less obvious.

REPLACING BROKEN WALL TILES

When a wall tile cracks or breaks, it needs careful removal with a hammer and chisel. You can replace a broken tile with a spare tile of the same colour, or alternatively you might fill the space with a decorated tile.

Wear thick gloves and safety goggles for protection and tap the tile with a hammer. Carefully remove each loose piece of the tile as it breaks off. Chisel out the old adhesive.

When the surface of the wall is clean, use a notched spreader to apply adhesive on to the back of the new tile. Do not apply too much adhesive or the tile may sit proud of the surrounding tiles. Fit the new tile in place, allow the adhesive to set, then fill in the gap around the tile with grout.

1 Tap the broken tile with a hammer protected by a cloth. It is a good idea to wear thick gloves and safety goggles to protect yourself from any sharp slivers that may splinter from the surface.

2 Working carefully from the hole outwards, use a hammer and cold chisel to remove pieces of the broken tile. Once the tile has been removed, chisel out any old adhesive from the wall.

3 Butter adhesive on to the back of a new tile, then slot it into place. Wipe the surface with a damp cloth and leave to set. After about 12 hours, fill in the gap around the new tile with grout.

WINDOWS &
DOORS

Because of their design and purpose, windows and doors can be subject to considerable wear and tear. Most are made of wood, which can become distorted with age and/or exposure to damp conditions. The latter can cause extensive damage to external doors and windows if they are not well maintained. Windows, and sometimes doors, also have the added weakness of glass. Being very brittle, this is easily broken, and knowing how to replace panels of glass yourself can save you a lot of money. Hinges can be a source of trouble in both windows and doors. Their screws can loosen, preventing the window or door from opening freely, and they can cause squeaks, rattles and binding. All of these problems are easily fixed.

REMOVING WINDOW GLASS

Removing broken window glass is a common do-it-yourself job, and something that is worth learning how to do properly.

Make sure you wear thick gloves that cover your wrists. Lay newspapers on the ground on both sides of the window. Collect the glass in newspaper or a cardboard box and dispose of it safely; your glass supplier may accept the broken pieces for recycling.

An old chisel can be used to chop out the old putty – do not use a good one, as its blade will be damaged by the sprigs (or clips in a metal frame) that hold the glass in place. Pull out the sprigs or clips and remove all the putty from the recess.

TIP

When removing broken glass from a window, apply a criss-cross pattern of adhesive tape to the pane to prevent the glass from flying around. For extra safety, grip the broken slivers of glass with a pair of pincers or pliers and pull them from the frame. Don't knock them out with a hammer.

1 Remove the broken glass, wearing gloves to prevent cuts.

2 Use an old chisel to remove the putty from the edges of the rebate.

3 Pull out the glazing sprigs with pincers. Then remove the remnants of glass and putty.

REPLACING LEADED LIGHTS

Replacing the glass in a leaded-light window is a little trickier than working with normal window panes. That said, it is a task well within the scope of anyone with patience and a practical frame of mind.

Many leaded-light windows will have one or more panes of coloured glass, so these will need to be replaced.

The best place to look for authentic coloured replacements is in an architectural salvage yard. A glass merchant can cut a piece of old glass down to size for you.

You will also need a really sharp trimming knife to cut through the lead cames at the corners, and a soldering iron to fuse the lead together.

1 Use a sharp trimming knife to cut through the cames at the corners at 45 degrees.

2 Lever up and fold back the cames all around the pane to remove the old glass.

3 With the new glass in place, press the cames back into place with a seam roller.

4 Fuse the lead together at the corners using a small electric soldering iron.

REPLACING WINDOW PANES

The first stage in replacing a window pane is to measure the size of the glass needed and then buy the new pane. Your supplier will be able to cut the glass to fit.

MEASURING UP
Take measurements of the width and height of the recess in several places. The size of glass you need is 3mm (⅛in) less than the size of the recess. If in doubt, cut a cardboard template to fit and take this with you to the glass supplier. Reckon on buying some new glazing sprigs or clips to hold the glass in place, and buy the correct putty for either wooden or metal windows.

PUTTING IN THE NEW GLASS
Take a small amount of putty and work it in your hands until it is pliable; if it sticks to your fingers, roll it out on newspaper to remove some of the oil. When it is workable, begin pressing a layer into the window recess, squeezing it out of the palm of your hand between thumb and forefinger rather like toothpaste.

Put the glass in place, resting it on a couple of wooden matches, and press it gently into the opening until putty is squeezed out at the back – press against the sides of the glass, not the centre. Then fit the glazing sprigs to hold the glass, sliding the head of the hammer across the surface of the glass,

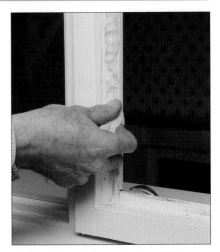

1 Knead the putty in your hands until it becomes workable. Then squeeze a thin layer into the rebate of the frame, feeding it from your palm between finger and thumb.

or re-fit the clips. Remove putty that has been squeezed out on the inside of the window.

Add more putty to the outside of the window, using the same thumb-and-forefinger technique, until you have a good bead all the way around the glass. Take a putty knife and smooth off this bead at an angle of 45 degrees, pushing the putty into the edges of the frame. If the knife sticks, wet it with water.

Leave the putty for about 14 days before painting over it to disguise and seal the joints, allowing the paint to overlap on to the glass to prevent moisture from seeping down into the frame.

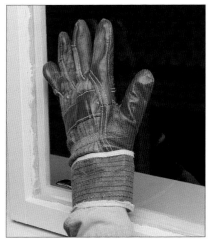

2 Support the bottom edge of the pane on a couple of wooden matches and press it into the putty, applying pressure to the sides rather than the centre.

3 Tap in the glazing sprigs at 300mm (12in) intervals. Hold the hammer so that its head slides across the face of the glass; that way, you will avoid breaking the glass.

4 Add more putty to the rebate and use the putty knife to strike it off to a 45-degree bevel. Make sure that the putty seals against the glass all round and that the sprigs are covered.

5 Trim the excess putty on the inside and outside of the frame to leave a neat finish. Allow the putty to harden before painting. Clean smears from the glass with methylated spirit.

REPAIRING WINDOWS

The most obvious signs that there is something wrong with a window are when it starts to rattle in the wind or to stick, making it difficult to open and close. Rattling is most likely to be caused by worn hinges or wear of the window itself; sticking by swelling of the wood, build-up of paint or movement of the frame joints.

REPAIRING HINGES

Loose or worn hinges are often a cause of window problems. To start with, try tightening the screws or replacing them with slightly longer screws of the same gauge. If that does not work, replace the hinges with new ones of the same size and type plus new screws. Remember that steel hinges will rust quickly, so apply suitable primer immediately, then repaint to match the window when this has dried.

Check the opening and closing of the window. If the window is sticking on the far edge, it may be necessary to deepen the recess for one or both hinges; if it binds on the closing edge, one or both recesses will be too deep and may need packing out with card. A rattling window can often be cured by fitting draught-excluder strip.

WORN WINDOWS

Sash windows are particularly prone to wear. The best answer is to remove the windows and fit brush-pile draught excluder inside the sash channel. A new catch to hold the windows together may also be necessary.

Fit a new inner staff bead around the window so that it fits more closely against the inner sash.

WARPED WINDOWS

Wooden hinged windows can sometimes warp so that they meet the frame only at the top or at the bottom. The best way to cure this is to fit some mortise window locks, which fit into holes cut in the casement, with the bolts shooting into more holes in the frame. These allow the window to be held in the correct position (get someone to push from the outside while you lock it) so that the warp will self-correct.

STICKING WINDOWS

Over time, a build-up of paint may cause windows to stick, especially when the weather is damp and the wood begins to swell. Use a plane to cut down the offending areas (this is much easier if you remove the window from its frame), then repaint before refitting the window.

Make sure that all bare wood is covered with paint, as this will prevent water from getting in, which causes the wood to swell. Also, check that the putty is in good condition.

TIP

When replacing painted steel hinges with brass versions, always use brass screws to match the new hinges.

ABOVE: A binding window may be cured simply by tightening the hinge screws or replacing them with longer ones.

ABOVE: If a window is binding on the far side, it may be that the hinge recesses need to be deepened with a chisel.

ABOVE: A sticking window may be swollen or have too much paint on it. Plane down the leading edge of the window.

ABOVE: A loose window joint can be re-glued with fresh adhesive. Clamp it up while the adhesive dries.

RE-HANGING DOORS

There may be occasions when the way in which a door opens is not the most convenient. Switching the hinges from one side to the other may provide a more attractive view of the room as the door is opened or allow better use of the wall space. Alternatively, making the door open outward may create more useful space. However, for safety, never have a door opening outward on to a stairway.

SWITCHING THE HINGED SIDE

When switching the hinged edge of a door from one side to the other, you will need to cut a new mortise for the latch and drill new holes for the door handle spindles. The old latch mortise and spindle holes can be filled by gluing in small blocks of wood and lengths of dowel. Leave the blocks and dowels slightly proud of the surface, then plane and sand them flush when the glue has dried. If you reverse the door, you will be able to use the old latch and door handle spindle holes, but the latch itself will need to be turned around.

You will need to cut a new slot for the striker and striking plate (keeper) on the other side of the frame, and fill the old recess with a thin block of wood stuck in place. Again, make this oversize, planing and sanding it flush once the adhesive has dried.

FILLING HINGE RECESSES

1 When switching the hinged side of a door, you will need to fill the old hinge recesses. Cut slivers of wood to the correct length and width, but slightly thicker than the recess depth.

REVERSING DOORS

When re-hanging a door, it can reduce the amount of work required if you reverse the door – that is, turn it so that the side which faced inward now faces outward. This is the case when changing the hinges from left to right or the other way round. There are, however, two problems with doing this. The first is that the two sides of the door may be painted in different colours, which will mean a complete re-painting job.

The second is that the door may not fit properly the other way round. Both doors and frames can move slightly over time, and while the door will operate perfectly well fitted one way,

2 Apply adhesive to each sliver of wood and tap it down into its recess. Wipe off excess adhesive with a damp cloth. Set the door aside for the adhesive to dry.

3 When the adhesive has set, use a jack plane to remove the wood that projects above the surface of the door edge. If necessary, fill any gaps around the slivers with wood filler.

 it may bind or catch when fitted the other way.

You will also need to chisel out new recesses for the hinges in both the door and the frame; if the door is reversed, you may be able to use part of the old hinge recesses in the door and need only fill the unused portions. Fill the old hinge recesses with thin blocks of wood glued into place and sanded flush.

If the door has rising butts or some other form of handed hinges, these will need to be replaced.

After re-hanging the door, the light switch may be in the wrong place if it is in the room the door opens into. There

are two choices here: reposition it on the other side of the door (which means running a new cable) or move it to the other side of the wall so that it is outside the room, but more or less in the same place (little or no new cable, but possible problems in securing the switch mounting box).

TIP

Modern honeycomb-cored internal doors are quite light in weight, but traditional panelled doors can be very heavy. If you are re-hanging such a door, make sure you have someone on hand to help lift it in and out of the opening.

CHANGING THE LATCH POSITION

1 Remove the existing door handle and latch from the door, along with the operating spindle. Cut a block of wood to fill the latch recess and glue it in place, wiping off excess glue with a damp cloth.

2 Plug the spindle hole on each side of the door by tapping in lengths of glued dowel. Fill all the screw holes with wood filler. When the glue and filler has dried, sand everything smooth.

OPENING IN TO OPENING OUT

When making a door open outward, you will be able to use the same latch and handle positions if the door is hung from the same side of the frame. You will have to reverse the latch, but will be able to make use of parts of the hinge recesses in the door. However, you will need to reposition the striking plate (keeper) and make new hinge recesses in the frame.

The one extra job will be to move the door stop, unless this is positioned centrally in the frame. Moving the door stop needs care to avoid splitting it – slide a chisel in behind the stop and lever it out. Remove the sides before the top, starting in the middle.

When repositioning the door stop, hang the door first, so that you can be sure that the stop fits snugly.

If you change the side of the frame from which the door is hung (as well as changing it from in to out), you can retain the existing door hinge, latch and door handle positions, although new recesses must still be cut in the frame for the hinges and striking plate.

TIP

To prevent the paint from chipping when you remove a door stop, run a trimming knife blade along the joint between door stop and frame to cut through the paint.

3 On the other side of the door, cut a recess in the edge for the latch and drill a hole for the spindle. You may need to drill another hole for a key if the latch is lockable.

4 Fit the latch and the operating spindle. Then add the handles. Fit hinges to the other side of the door and cut recesses in the frame for the hinges and striking plate (keeper).

REPOSITIONING THE DOOR STOP

1 After cutting through the paint film, carefully slide a chisel under the door stop and gently prise it from the frame. Remove the old nails.

2 Drill new nail clearance holes in the stop and nail it to the door frame in its new position. Fill all the nail holes before re-painting.

REPAIRING DOORS

Doors can develop all sorts of problems, from simple squeaks and rattles to suddenly refusing to open and shut properly. Fortunately, most of the problems are easy to solve, although for most repairs you will need to remove the door from the frame.

SQUEAKS

A door normally squeaks simply because the hinges need oiling. Often you can dribble sufficient oil on to the hinges with the door in place, but if they are caked in dirt and paint, it is best to remove the door and work the hinges back and forth with oil.

A door may also squeak if the hinges are binding, usually because the recesses have been cut too deep into the door and/or frame. To cure this problem, unscrew each half of each hinge in turn, place a piece of cardboard behind the hinge, then refit the screws.

RATTLES

The simplest way to stop any door rattling is to fit a draught excluder. With an internal door, you could also try moving the door stop; with all types of door, you could try moving the latch striking plate, although this is not easy – drilling out and filling the old screw holes with glued-in dowels helps.

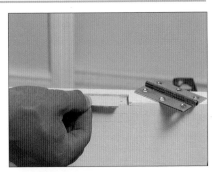

ABOVE: You can fix a squeaking hinge by unscrewing each half of the hinge in turn and packing the recess with cardboard.

WARPED DOORS

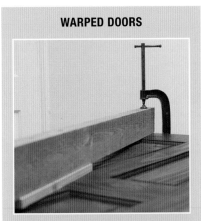

If a door has become warped, you can straighten it with pairs of clamps, stout lengths of wood and packing blocks. Mount the door between the timbers, say lengths of 50 x 100mm (2 x 4in), and position the packing blocks to force the door in the opposite direction to the warp. Force it beyond straight by tightening up the clamps and leave for as long as you can. When the clamps are removed, the door should be straight.

BINDING

External doors often bind during cold, damp weather, becoming free again when the weather is dry and warm. This is a sign that the bottom of the door was not sealed when the door was painted, allowing moisture to get in.

Binding doors can also be caused by a build-up of paint on the leading (non-hinge) edge. The cure is to remove the door and plane down the leading edge, re-painting it once the door has been fitted. Add primer to the bottom of the door to prevent more moisture from getting in.

If a door binds at the bottom, it may be because the hinges have worked loose. Try tightening the screws, fitting larger or longer screws if necessary. If this does not work, remove the door and plane down the part that is rubbing.

A door can bind seriously when you have fitted a new floorcovering. In this case, remove the door and cut a strip off the bottom with a door trimming saw.

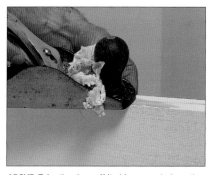

ABOVE: Take the door off its hinges and plane the leading (non-hinge) edge if it is binding.

ABOVE: Fit longer screws to a hinge if the old ones have lost their grip.

ABOVE: Running the base of a door over abrasive paper may be enough to cure binding.

ABOVE: You can hire a door trimming saw to adjust the height after fitting a new carpet.

FLOORS & STAIRS

Of all the surfaces in your home, the floors take the most punishment. The continual passage of people to and fro, plus the scraping of furniture can cause substantial damage over time. In addition to day-to-day wear, wooden floors can also be attacked by rot and insects, with damage extending to the supporting structure of joists below. Older wooden floors invariably have individual boards that may warp, crack and shrink, opening up gaps that lead to draughts. Solid floors may develop cracks or be uneven, while floor coverings such as tiles and carpet can suffer from a variety of ills. Stairs are subject to heavy wear, too, as a result of which their joints can become loose and their treads broken.

LIFTING FLOORBOARDS

The majority of floors in older homes will have individual floorboards nailed to supporting joists. In modern homes, sheets of flooring-grade chipboard (particle board) will be nailed or screwed to the joists. If a new floorcovering is to be laid, it is essential that the floor is in good condition. If floorboards are to be exposed, they must be in even better condition, as any defects will be visible.

To inspect the underfloor space or fit new floorboards, you will need to lift existing floorboards. You may find some that have been cut and lifted in the past to provide access to pipes or cables. These should be easy to lever up with a bolster (stonecutter's) chisel – do not use a screwdriver as you will damage the floorboard.

To lift boards that have not been cut, check first that they are not tongued-and-grooved – a tongue along one edge of each board fitting into a groove along the adjacent edge of its neighbour. If they are, use a floorboard saw or a circular saw with its cutting depth set to 20mm (¾in) to cut through the tongues.

Lever up the floorboard with your bolster, and use a floorboard saw to make a right-angled cut across it. Make the cut exactly over a joist so that the two parts of the board will be supported when they are replaced.

Chipboard sheets are easy to unscrew, but you may need to cut through tongues in the same manner as for traditional floorboards to be able to lift them.

1 If the board is tongued-and-grooved, cut through the tongue with a circular saw. Lift the end of the floorboard by levering with a bolster (stonecutter's) chisel.

2 Use wooden wedges to keep the end of the board raised. Check that there are no pipes or cables underneath and cut through it above the centre of a joist with a floorboard saw.

JOIST PROBLEMS

Most of the problems associated with floor joists are due to dampness, which may occur if airbricks (vents) have become blocked or if there are not enough airbricks to ensure adequate ventilation of the underfloor space.

Lift a few floorboards and inspect the joists with a torch and a mirror, prodding any suspect areas with a bradawl. If sections of joist are damaged, you should be able to cut and lift floorboards or chipboard (particle board) sheets over the damage and bolt on a new section of joist of the same size, making sure that it is fixed to solid wood. Do not bother to remove the old joist unless it is actually rotten. If you do find signs of dry rot (typically white strands), all damaged wood must be removed by a firm of professionals. If you find signs of woodworm attack, treat the affected areas with a recommended woodworm eradicator or call in a professional firm.

If you want to strengthen a floor so that it will support a partition wall running directly above a joist, you can sandwich the existing joist between two reinforcing joists. These should be supported at each end by metal joist hangers screwed to the wallplate or masonry and butted up to the existing joist. Cut the new joists to length, drop them into the hangers and drill holes through all three joists at 900mm (3ft) intervals. Pass 12mm (½in) bolts through the holes and tighten.

1 Cut the new joist section to length and clamp it in place while you drill holes through it and through the old joist. A right-angled drill attachment makes this easy.

2 Fit washers beneath the bolt heads, pass them through the holes and add another washer beneath each nut before tightening them with an adjustable spanner.

REPAIRING WOOD FLOORS

A wood floor should have a sound and smooth surface. Even if the wood is covered by carpet or tiles, any faults not rectified will eventually show through any floorcovering and may damage it. It is therefore essential that you fill holes, cracks and gaps, as well as make the surface level and smooth.

FILLING HOLES

Nail and screw holes can easily be plugged using a flexible wood filler applied with a filling or putty knife. If the floorboards are to be left exposed and treated with a clear sealer, try to match the wood filler, or stopping, to the colour of the surrounding floorboards – so carry out the filling after any sanding.

Larger recesses can also be filled with flexible filler, but if a knot has fallen out, leaving a large round hole, plug this by gluing in a short length of dowel and planing it smooth when the glue has dried. Select a dowel that matches the colour of the floor or stain it once planed down.

FILLING CRACKS

You will find two main kinds of crack in wood floors: splits in the ends of the floorboards and gaps between the boards.

A split can often be cured by skew (toe) nailing – i.e., driving two nails through the end of the board at an angle toward the centre and down into the joist. As the nails are driven in, they should close up the split.

Gaps between floorboards are more difficult to deal with. If they are narrow, flexible wood filler will work, but for wider gaps, you must cut slivers of wood and glue them into place in the gaps. Once the glue has dried, plane or sand the slivers flush with the surrounding floor and stain to match.

If there are lots of wide gaps between floorboards, a better solution is to lift all the floorboards one by one, starting at one side of the room and working toward the other, and re-lay them tightly against one another. Floorboard clamps will help you do this, as they force a board against its neighbour while you nail or screw it down.

LEVELLING A WOOD FLOOR

Individual rough patches on a wood floor can be sanded down by hand, but where floorboards have become cupped or are heavily encrusted with old paint, grease and polish, the best move is to hire an industrial-type sanding machine and re-sand the floor. Begin with coarse abrasive and progress through to the fine grades, working across the floorboards at an angle. Finish off by working along the boards with fine abrasive. Hire an edging sander as well, unless you own a belt sander, because the floor sander will not sand right up to the skirtings (baseboards).

FILLING GAPS BETWEEN FLOORBOARDS

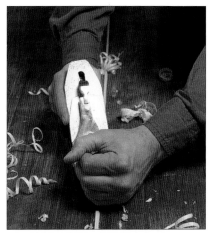

1 Drive glued slivers of wood between floorboards to fill large gaps. Leave them just proud of the surrounding boards, wipe off excess glue with a damp cloth and allow the glue to dry.

2 Plane down the wood slivers flush with the floor when the glue has dried. If the floorboards are to be left exposed, stain the slivers so that they match the colour of the boards.

FILLING HOLES AND SPLITS

ABOVE: Use flexible wood filler to cover the holes made by nail heads and screws.

ABOVE: With a split board, glue the split, then drive in nails at an angle to close it up.

FITTING NEW FLOORBOARDS

Over a period of time, floorboards can develop a number of faults. The natural flexing of the wood as it is walked on can begin to loosen nails, leading to squeaks and creaks. If sections are lifted regularly, they can be damaged, or the wood may simply warp and split with age.

LOOSE FLOORBOARDS

If floorboards are loose, the best answer is to replace the nails holding them down with screws. Do not put a screw in the middle of a board – there could be a pipe underneath. If nail heads are protruding, use a hammer and nail punch to set them below the surface of the floorboards. This is essential before attempting to use a sanding machine or laying carpet or sheet vinyl.

DAMAGED FLOORBOARDS

If floorboards are split or broken, the damaged section, at least, will need to be replaced. The most likely problem is that old floorboards will have become "cupped", or turned up at the edges. You can overcome this by hiring a floor sanding machine.

You do not need to replace a whole floorboard if only part of it is damaged; simply lift the board and cut out the damaged section, making the cuts over the centres of joists.

FITTING FLOORBOARDS

ABOVE: Plane down a floorboard if it is too wide to fill the gap.

If a replacement floorboard is too wide, plane it down to fit the gap – do not fit a narrower replacement floorboard, as this will result in draughts. If the board is slightly thicker, chisel slots out of it where it fits over the joists; if it is thinner, use packing

FIXING FLOORBOARDS

ABOVE: Drill pilot holes for floorboard nails to avoid splitting the wood.

ABOVE: Use card or plywood packing pieces over the joists if the board is too shallow.

ABOVE: Use a chisel to cut slots to fit over joists if the board is too thick.

pieces of cardboard or plywood between the joists and the board. Secure each floorboard with two floorboard nails at each joist, positioning them about 25mm (1in) from the edge of the board and exactly in the middle of the joist. It is a good idea to drill pilot holes in the board first.

TIP

When laying new floorboards, make sure that you can still gain access to pipes and cables underneath. If necessary, cut removable inspection hatches in both the floor and any new floorcoverings.

ABOVE: Hammer down protruding nails to prevent them from damaging the floorcovering.

ABOVE: Secure loose floorboards by replacing the nails with screws.

REPAIRING SOLID FLOORS

Provided a solid floor is basically sound and dry, you should be able to fill cracks and holes using a quick-set repair mortar. All loose material should be removed and the cracks enlarged if necessary to give the mortar something to grip.

The surface of the crack or hole should be brushed with a solution of one part PVA (white) glue and five parts water to reduce absorbency and help the mortar adhere to the floor. Use the same PVA glue and water solution to make up the mortar, then trowel it into place, building up two or more layers in a deep hole. Level the surface with a plasterer's trowel.

DEALING WITH DAMP

Concrete floors should incorporate a damp-proof membrane to prevent moisture from rising up from the ground below. However, it is possible that this may have broken down, or not have been incorporated at all. To check for rising damp, lay a piece of polythene (polyethylene) sheet on the floor and seal its edges with tape. After a couple of days, moisture should be visible on the underside of the sheet if the condition exists. To protect against rising damp, paint the floor with two or three coats of a waterproofing compound. When it has dried, floorcoverings can be laid on top, or a self-levelling compound added.

1 After opening out a crack in a solid floor and brushing out all debris and dust, brush the surfaces with a solution of PVA (white) glue to help the new mortar bond to it.

2 Mix a small amount of quick-set repair mortar, again using PVA solution, and work it into the crack with a small trowel. Smooth the mortar flush with the surrounding floor and leave to harden.

LEVELLING SOLID FLOORS

Little skill is required to produce a smooth, flat, solid floor surface, as a self-levelling floor compound will do the job for you.

Before you start, clear the room, removing all skirtings (baseboards) and doors; nail battens across thresholds to prevent the compound from spreading. Fill any cracks or holes more than 6mm (¼in) deep and brush the floor with the PVA (white) glue/water solution. Mix the floor levelling compound in a bucket and tip it out on to the floor, spreading it with a plasterer's trowel or a float. Leave it to settle. Once the compound has dried, you can refit the skirtings and doors, but check that the latter will clear the higher floor when opened.

1 If the floor is excessively porous, seal it by brushing on a coat of diluted PVA (white) glue. Then mix up the self-levelling floor compound according to the manufacturer's instructions.

2 Starting from the corner farthest from the door, pour the compound on to the floor. Do not pour too much on to the floor at any one time, otherwise you will not be able to reach across it.

3 Using a plasterer's trowel, smooth the compound to a thickness of approximately 3mm (⅛in). Allow at least 24 hours for the compound to dry before walking on it.

REPAIRING FLOOR TILES

Of all the types of floorcovering, tiled finishes can be the easiest to repair, since individual tiles can often be lifted and replaced. The way you do it depends on whether the tile is hard or soft and on how it has been secured to the floor. Even damaged carpet can be patched effectively, but care needs to be taken to avoid further damage to surrounding areas.

Ceramic and quarry tiles are among the most difficult tiles to replace, as first you will have to chip out the old tile. Drill a few holes in the tile with the biggest masonry drill you own, then use a club (spalling) hammer and small bolster (stonecutter's) chisel

to chip out the tile, making sure you do not damage the surrounding tiles. Chip out all old adhesive or mortar and grout from the hole.

Lay some new tile adhesive (for ceramic tiles) or mortar (for quarry tiles) and push the replacement tile gently into place. If it is not flush with its neighbours, lift it quickly and add or remove adhesive or mortar as necessary. Clean any excess mortar or adhesive off the face of the tile and leave to set before making good the gaps around the tile with grout (ceramic tiles) or more mortar (quarry tiles). If re-laying several tiles, it helps if you make up some small spacers.

1 Remove any cracked quarry or ceramic tiles with a club (spalling) hammer and small bolster (stonecutter's) chisel. Wear gloves to protect your hands, and safety goggles to shield your eyes.

2 Bed a new quarry tile on mortar, but use the recommended adhesive for a ceramic tile. Level the tile with its neighbours using a strip of wood; wipe off excess mortar or adhesive.

REPAIRING WOODEN MOSAIC TILES

There are two ways to replace wooden mosaic tiles. One is to lift the whole tile, which consists of four groups of timber strips, and replace it with a new one. First drill or chisel out one strip, then lever the rest of the tile from the floor. The second method is to remove just the damaged strip or strips and glue in replacements taken from a spare tile, pressing them into place with a block of wood.

If the new strip sits a little proud of its neighbours, it should be sanded down, using abrasive paper and a sanding block, until it lies flush. Then sand the entire tile and re-varnish it. If the tiles are pre-finished, you will have to sand the back of the strip before gluing it.

1 First drill a sequence of closely spaced holes through the damaged mosaic strip, stopping each when you just break through the wood. Take care not to allow the drill to wander.

2 Carefully cut away the strip, working outward from the holes with a narrow-bladed chisel held bevel down. Do not let the chisel slip when you approach the edges of adjoining strips.

3 Apply a little adhesive to the new mosaic strip and place it carefully in position, taking care not to get adhesive on the adjoining strips. Using a block of wood and a hammer, tap it down.

REPLACING SOFT FLOOR TILES

Most soft floor tiles – vinyl, cork, lino and rubber – are replaced in the same way. First you have to soften the adhesive holding the tile in place, which is best done with a hot-air gun, starting at one corner and gradually peeling the tile back. This becomes easier once you can direct the hot-air gun beneath the tile. An old chisel can be used to remove any remaining adhesive. Check that the replacement tile is an exact fit.

Some soft tiles are self-adhesive, requiring only the removal of backing paper, while others require a separate adhesive. Always add the adhesive to the back of a replacement tile to avoid staining the other tiles.

With the adhesive in place, or the backing paper removed, hold the tile against the edge of one of the surrounding tiles and lower it into place. You may only get one attempt at this, so take care to get it right.

TIP

If you do not have any spare tiles and are unable to obtain a matching colour or pattern for the existing flooring, consider replacing the damaged tile with one of a contrasting colour or pattern. To disguise the repair, replace a few of the undamaged tiles with similar contrasting tiles, setting them out in a regular or random pattern. If you cannot find tiles of the correct size, buy larger ones and carefully cut them down to fit.

1 Remove a vinyl or cork tile using a hot-air gun to soften the adhesive. Work a scraper under the edge and gradually prise the tile from the floor.

2 Apply adhesive to the back of the replacement vinyl or cork tile, set one edge in place against its neighbour and lower it in place.

PATCHING CARPET

Provided you have a matching piece, you can patch most types of carpet, but it may be worth cleaning the carpet first, since the patch could be a brighter colour. First decide how large the patch should be – if the carpet is patterned, you may want to join along a pattern line – cut the patch about 25mm (1in) larger than this all round, with the same part of any pattern. Lay the patch over the carpet, lining up the pattern exactly, and secure it with adhesive tape.

Using a trimming knife fitted with a new blade and a metal straightedge, make a single cut down through both thicknesses of carpet along each edge of the patch. Remove the tape and lift both pieces of carpet – the patch should fit exactly into the hole in the carpet with the pattern matching.

With foam-backed carpet, lay double-sided tape on the floor around the edges of the hole so that each strip overlaps the joint between the old carpet and the patch. Brush the edges

of the patch and the hole with latex adhesive to prevent fraying, then press the carpet patch on to the tape. Remove excess adhesive with a damp cloth.

With fabric-backed carpet, use non-adhesive carpet repair tape and latex adhesive on the back and edges of the patch and the hole. Press the patch down into the hole with a wallpaper seam roller and wipe off any excess adhesive with a damp cloth.

1 Use a trimming knife and straightedge to cut through both the patch and the existing carpet to ensure an exact fit.

2 Press the carpet patch on to double-sided adhesive tape. Brush the edges with latex adhesive to prevent fraying.

3 The finished patch of carpet should fit exactly into the hole and the seams should be invisible in long-pile carpet.

CURING STAIRCASE PROBLEMS

A timber staircase consists of a series of evenly spaced horizontal treads that form the flight. Most staircases also have vertical risers, which fill the space between the rear edge of one tread and the front edge of the tread above; these may be nailed in place, or may have tongued edges that slot into grooves in the treads.

The treads are supported at each side by two parallel beams called strings. A closed-string staircase has the treads and risers set into grooves cut in the inner faces of the strings, while an open-string staircase has the outer string cut in a zigzag fashion so the treads can rest on the cutouts. The inner string – the one against the wall of the stairwell – is always a closed string.

At the open side of a conventional flight, a guard is fitted to run between the top and bottom newel posts – main uprights supporting flight. This usually consists of a series of closely-spaced balusters, which are fixed between the top edge of the outer string and the underside of a handrail, but it may be a solid panelled barrier. There may also be a wall-mounted handrail at the other side of the flight; freestanding flights must obviously have a balustrade at each side.

Stairs creak because one of the components has become loose; a footfall then causes the loose part to move against an adjacent component of the flight. A cure is simple if the underside of the flight is accessible, but less straightforward if it is not.

1 If there is no access to the underside of the flight, secure loose or squeaking treads by fixing metal repair brackets to tread and riser. If the underside can be reached, check that the wedges securing the treads and risers to the strings are in place. Hammer them in firmly if they are loose.

4 Insert a crowbar (wrecking bar) between the string and the tread, and prise it up and out to free it from the risers above and below it. Mark out and cut a replacement. Plane the nosing to shape, and cut notches in one end for the balusters.

2 Glue back any of the support blocks beneath the fronts of the treads if they have fallen off. Fit extra blocks beneath troublesome treads. Drill clearance holes up through the rear edge of each tread, then drive screws up into the bottom edge of the riser above to lock the tread to it.

3 If the tread is found to be split, it must be replaced. Start by prising off the side moulding, then tap the balusters out with a mallet. Insert a knife into the joint along the back of the tread to check if it has been nailed or screwed. If it has, use a hacksaw blade to cut the fixings.

5 Glue and clamp support blocks to the rear face of the riser below, and nail another block to the closed string to provide extra support for the replacement tread.

6 Fit the new tread in place and secure it to the support blocks and to the cutout in the open string with screws rather than nails. With the tread securely fixed in position, replace the balusters in their notches and nail the side moulding back on.

INDEX